LIKE UNTO

Where Took Place the Incidents

CALOOSAHATCHEE RIVER

KEY WEST

TEN THOUSAND ISLANDS

SEMINOLE INDIANS

SPANISH CHANNEL

SHARK RIVER

THE EVERGLADES

"PETER"

ENGLISHMAN ISLAND

PORTUGUESE MAN-O'WAR

MOO

Voyage

LIKE UNTO

A Philosophical Review

of a Vacation Journey

on Strange Waters

DONE AS A CHRISTMAS GIFT
FOR HIS FRIENDS
BY J.L.KRAFT · 1939

The Parable of

A DREAM WHICH CAME TRUE

IN the land of dreams and wishes there once lived a family of three; husband, wife and daughter. Now these three, dwelling together in peace and harmony and the fear of God as a family should, developed through the years a similarity of likes and dislikes, of dreams dreamed together.

Among these dreams a favored one was of open water and of setting sail on some enchanted voyage. For many years they discussed in the family circle the possibility of acquiring a small ship on which to make a vagabond voyage. Of all the charts they studied diligently, and with which they filled their dreams, those which outlined the inland waterway of the State of Florida most pleased them. And as the years passed, one following the other, an understanding developed that, should the longed-for voyage ever become reality, its course should follow that winding waterway.

5

The wish for that vagabond voyage continued to be only a hope of fading vagueness until it was learned that a friend of the city of Norfolk was possessed of a ship of the requisite dimensions, which he was with the utmost kindness willing to charter for such a voyage. The name of this ship was the Gypsy, truly a fitting name for a vessel vagabond. Forty-eight feet in length overall, eleven feet of beam, she possessed a draft sufficiently shallow to allow navigation in the low waters of the rivers, streams, inland lakes, and among the ten thousand islands off the southern Everglades of that intricate course.

Accordingly, all arrangements completed, the family of three, together with Captain Green and Frank, cook and keeper of the ship, set sail from the city of Jacksonville, upon the waters of the St. Johns River. Friends came aboard the Gypsy from time to time, to share this voyage wrought of much wishing, but other than this family and crew none sailed the entire journey.

From first to last, the Gypsy sailed a distance of about one thousand five hundred miles, following principally the inland waterways and proceeding hither and yon, seeking out-of-the-way waters where other ships went not. Be it known to all that enjoyment was complete beyond the anticipation thereof, and that even though mishaps occurred, the common lot of sailors everywhere, a dream did come true. Further than this, many new lessons were learned, and many old lessons were learned anew, some of which are recorded hereafter.

The fulfillment of this dream voyage is like unto a parable which is recorded in Holy Writ in the eleventh chapter of Luke wherein a certain man desiring assistance begged of a friend many times over that it be granted.

It is recorded that the wish was granted, not because of friendship but out of the man's great importunity. Further it is recorded, "And I say unto you, ask, and it shall be given you; seek and ye shall find; knock and it shall be opened unto you."

The Parable of

THE BROKEN CLUTCH

"THE wind bloweth where it listeth and thou hearest the sound thereof but canst not tell whence it cometh or whither it goeth." (John 3:8).

Not so does the wind have its will with a ship which is propelled by an engine, for therein are many pieces of machinery aptly fitted together and synchronized in their movements in such way that when levers are operated properly the ship will move forward even in the teeth of a gale.

However, if any single part of the machinery fails to do its duty, all parts fail together; likewise if each part does its duty, all will function perfectly.

Now it so happens that one of the vital parts of an engine is the clutch. The clutch is attached to the driving shaft of the engine and when certain levers are shifted, the gears upon the driving shaft mesh with the gears upon the clutch, which in turn engages the propeller shaft. Thus the propeller shaft turns, and thus the ship moves forward or backward at the will of the man at the controls.

On a certain morning when the Gypsy prepared to sail from the port of Jacksonville, it was discovered that the clutch was broken so that, even when engaged with the propeller shaft in the proper manner for operation, it was without force and the Gypsy moved neither forward nor backward until necessary repairs had been made.

The broken clutch, impeding the progress of the ship, is like unto a man in a high place—a statesman, minister, or executive with responsibility—who fails to function in his proper place. He may be led astray by those who advocate a false doctrine and thus become ineffectual, inoperative, impeding progress within his entire sphere of influence, until such time as he is cast aside or brought back into gear with the rest of the mechanism of society.

The Parable of

THE BUOY
WHICH BROKE AWAY

AT the place where the Halifax River empties into the canal leading into the St. Johns River there is a narrow channel which, to negotiate without mishap, requires the skill of the experienced navigator. In order to assist mariners, the Coast Guard has placed at the north entrance of this difficult channel a floating buoy which, though it bobs like a cork on the top of the water, is yet anchored fast by its submerged portion. If the wind blows a gale, the buoy is tossed on the waves wildly, to such an extent that a bell attached to the top of the buoy is automatically sounded. Thus are the pilots of oncoming ships, which may sail that way by night, warned of danger.

Now it so happened that just before the time when the Gypsy sailed that way, a storm arose, the force of which was so great that the anchor chain holding the floating buoy to its moorings broke away, and the buoy drifted to the shoal waters hard by. As the Gypsy approached, the pilot, having no knowledge that the buoy had drifted, steered by its false position and thus the Gypsy ran aground. There she remained fast until high tide permitted her to float free and proceed.

The anchorless buoy is like unto many a false sign-post along the straight and narrow channel leading to success. A young man embarking upon a career—professional, commercial, or political—fixes his ambition upon a distant goal, his path extending along the straight line of honesty, truth, and Christian principles. But as he proceeds, the way seems far, and certain men persuade him that the anchorless buoys which they themselves pursue lead straighter to his goal. And if the young man should deviate from his course, should fail to follow the hard and fast rules of navigation, by instruments which he knows to be sound, yet will he find to his despair that he has been deceived and led to his destruction.

The Parable of

THE ST. LUCIE LOCK

SEVERAL leagues from the area where Mosquito Lagoon merges into the Indian River is situated the palm studded little city of Stuart. Here it is that the St. Lucie River flows also into the Indian River. Navigators sailing westward to the Gulf of Mexico enter the St. Lucie at this point, following the river and come into Lake Okeechobee.

Since Florida is without hills or valleys, a strange situation confronts the navigator who would travel on the waters of Lake Okeechobee, for this lake is many feet above the natural surface of the waters of the St. Lucie by which it is approached. (This curious situation is more fully explained in the Parable of Lake Okeechobee.)

Briefly, in order for a ship to proceed on its course beyond the St. Lucie River, it is necessary that it be lifted up to a level with the surface of Lake Okeechobee. The

13

device for accomplishing this is called a lock. The lock is a massive construction of masonry and iron. It is built in the form of a great enclosure or box across the waters of the river, and upon either end are fitted ponderous gates of steel.

If a ship is proceeding westward, the gate on the St. Lucie end of the lock is opened and the ship proceeds into the confines of the lock. The gates are then closed on the St. Lucie end and slowly opened on the Lake Okeechobee end of the lock. As these gates are opened, the waters from the higher level of the lake flow into the lock until it is filled with water to the level of the lake above. Thus as the water rises, the ship is lifted with it; and when the upper gates are open she sails away.

The operation of the St. Lucie Lock is like unto the long-time planning of a business man. At the beginning of his career, though the sailing may not be easy, the problems of navigation are comparatively simple ones. Yet far ahead and above him, if he is wise, he sees upper reaches which he must gain, by skill and careful planning. Therefore, day after day he prepares himself for his future by building a strong lock of reserves which are physical, mental, and spiritual. Thus when the test comes, he is able to raise himself up to the levels of new opportunities.

The Parable of

LAKE OKEECHOBEE

N about the geographical center of Florida, between the east and west boundaries, lies a large body of
fresh water called Lake Okeechobee. By reason of the
fact that all the flood waters from as far north as Georgia,
following the natural water courses, eventually drain
into this lake, great floods have occurred there from
time immemorial. These floods wrought havoc, the more
so because the lake itself had no well-defined limits. As
rains descended, the waters overflowed the low lying
banks, doing much damage to life and property.

To solve this problem came competent engineers, men
of foresight and vision. Forthwith they measured and
calculated and planned to the end that a dyke was built
completely surrounding Lake Okeechobee. Many feet
high was this dyke, so high, in fact, that when the heavy
rains flowed down from the north, all the flood waters
could be held within the well-defined area of the dyke.

Thus is presented the peculiar phenomenon of a lake whose surface is often eighteen feet above the surrounding area. Yet life and property are now secure from floods; prosperity and happiness abide where once was uncertainty and desolation.

The building of the dyke is like unto a tempestuous man who learns to control his own nature. Before he has built defenses within his own character, he disregards personal and property rights of his fellow-men, rides over them rough-shod. But oft-times, brought low by his own destructive methods, having suffered bitter disappointments, he learns his lesson, and by controlling himself serves best himself and others.

The Parable of

THE UNCHARTED WATERS

AT the place where the St. Lucie Canal empties into Lake Okeechobee, the Coast Guard survey officers have placed on a prominent headland a large sign which reads: "He who sails beyond this point does so at his own risk." For it is known that the waters of this lake, under the stress of gale, become so violent that floating buoys are washed away, and because of the constant shifting of the bottom of the lake, permanent markers are impractical. Therefore, he who sails Lake Okeechobee must depend entirely upon his compass.

Now the lake is a very large body of water, and during the period of crossing it no land is in sight for a considerable distance. As the Gypsy sailed upon its broad expanse, and during the time when its shores were invisible, a storm arose. It was a violent gale such as descends without warning in the region thereabout. Clouds blotted out the sun, and the wind howled fierce through the guy ropes of the mast. Darkness shrouded the waves as they dashed high and tossed the Gypsy about like a chip of wood upon the waters.

During the period of the greatest violence of the storm, it seemed doubtful whether the Gypsy could make port because of the lack of buoys or markers. However, the Captain was of a calm and serene demeanor, and when approached he spoke as follows: "Have no fear. The compass is tested, the charts are true. If the Gypsy continues to sail southwest by south as she now sets, she will sail directly into the mouth of the Caloosahatchee River within the period of ninety minutes."

And it was so as he had said.

The Captain in his calm faith is like unto any God-fearing man who, having laid down a plan of life which he is convinced is the right course, having tested his compass and his charts, continues on his way. Though the winds may blow and the waves become mountainous, he is sure in his hope of the goal.

The Parable of

THE YOUNG WOMAN

THERE sailed upon the Gypsy a young woman whose name is Edith, comely and possessed of much of that which is generally called common sense.

Now as the Gypsy sailed the unmarked waters of Lake Okeechobee, a storm arose. So violent was the storm that the Gypsy was tossed hither and yon, now plunging down into the trough of the waves, and again mounting to their crest. As the storm had its will with the Gypsy, objects on the ship were tossed about, and furniture was driven from place to place until it was quite impossible for the ship's passengers to sit or stand in any elected spot.

The wise young woman spoke as follows to her fellow-voyagers: "The storm has descended on us. The sky is overcast, with lowering clouds, and I have been unable to find a stable place of refuge. But I perceive, as I look into the heavens, a bright spot, where it is evident the sunlight is beating upon the dark clouds in an effort to penetrate them. I will therefore sit on the open deck and gaze upon that bright spot, for has it not ever been so that light follows the darkness? I will then have beneath me the solid teakwood planking of the good ship Gypsy, and above me a bright spot from the heavens, which must soon overcome the darkness."

Accordingly she did as she had said, and in a short space of time the whole earth was filled with sunlight and the storm had disappeared, even as she had said.

She was like unto the Christian man or woman who, living in this stormy world, filled with black wars and rumors of wars, with strife and clouds of doubt descending all about, still looks upon the light from heaven, calm in the faith that light will disperse the darkness.

The Parable of

THE MOORE HAVEN LOCK

S IT is stated in the Parable of Lake Okeechobee, the surface waters of Lake Okeechobee are substantially higher than the country which surrounds the lake. Therefore, ships sailing either westward or eastward or indeed in any direction from this body of water must be lowered to the earth's normal level.

Sailing westward toward Fort Myers, on the Gulf of Mexico, as was her course, the Gypsy arrived after nightfall at the Moore Haven Lock, which is a place of exit into the Caloosahatchee River.

The great iron and concrete gates at the lake end of the lock being already open, the Gypsy sailed quietly between the stone walls of Moore Haven Lock. While cables were being attached to restrain the Gypsy from drifting during the evacuation of the lock, the great gates closed upon the upper water level. Simultaneously, the gates on the lower level end of the lock slowly opened, allowing the water within the lock to flow into the Caloosahatchee below. After this process of levelling off the waters was completed, the Gypsy proceeded on her course up the river, at the normal water level.

The levelling off at the Moore Haven Lock is like unto the realization a man comes to after he has known a mountain-top experience: the heights of inspiration are stimulating, thrilling; but to navigate his ship successfully through life, it is best in the main not to travel too far above his fellows. (Or if he sails high waters, let him see to it that a Moore Haven Lock is at hand to bring him back to normal level.)

The Parable of

THE HERMIT

ALMOST due south of the small city of Naples, on the shore of the Gulf of Mexico toward the southwestern extremity of Florida, there lies a gem of an island called Marco. Marco is the largest and most northerly of the group known as the Ten Thousand Islands.

Now it so happened that the Gypsy sailed into the miniature fishing port of Marco Island in the early afternoon, to take on fuel and fresh water. But as the day was well-nigh spent, it was deemed wise to proceed no further until the morrow.

Among many fascinating islands in that region was one known as Tices Island. And it was discovered that there dwelt thereon a hermit who had withdrawn from human society, and who supplied practically all of his meager needs from the tiny area of land upon which he lived.

It was thought well to visit this hermit and to learn whether perhaps he possessed secrets of value to the great body of his fellow-men. A fisherman volunteered his services for this expedition, and in a small skiff successfully negotiated a passage of five miles, bringing up at Tices Island at sunset.

The island was indeed a place of great beauty, thickly grown with palm trees. In the center of the grove sat a dilapidated one-room cabin, built of rough driftwood gathered from the beach. Joe, the hermit, appeared upon the beach to extend a cordial welcome. Except for a pair of once-blue overalls, tattered, above knee-length, the hermit was innocent of clothing. He lived alone in most primitive fashion, cooking his food in an iron kettle over an outdoor fire, and sleeping inside his box of a house on a rude bench covered with meager bedding.

His occupation was gathering shells which he shipped periodically to a far-away city. But, according to his own words, he had no use for the money which they brought. He simply gathered shells to provide occupation. He had persuaded himself, and so stated, that he had solved all the problems of life, and it was his intent to live out his days on Tices Island.

He was like unto the monks of old, who took their vows, then withdrew unto mountain monasteries away from the world, to the end that they might become, to their own minds, truly holy men. They too believed that they had solved the problems of life. Yet when they withdrew they were not missed, and when they died, no one knew they were gone. Verily no problems did they solve. Withdrawing from the world, they merely avoided their responsibility to their fellows and to society in general.

The Parable of

THE FALSE GUIDE

NOW there are certain waters due south of Florida in which are situated the Ten Thousand Islands, and extending northward from the shoreline, over a vast expanse of the mainland, lie the Everglades. This is a swampy region, through which certain rivers run. The largest of these is called Shark River.

In this region Seminole Indians dwell, but few, if any, white men find habitation there. In the upper reaches of the Shark River are the rookeries of uncounted millions of egrets and other rare and colorful birds. So difficult of navigation are channels into this region that none excepting those native to these surroundings are able to pilot ships with safety through the waters. Therefore, a pilot who professed to be entirely familiar with the channels and shoals was engaged to direct the Gypsy to the head waters of the Shark River.

All went well during the journey through the Ten

25

Thousand Islands and the wide reaches of the Shark River where the channels were well defined. But upon reaching that portion of the river which divides into many channels, only one of which is navigable, it became apparent that the pilot was not as experienced as he professed to be. For he piloted the Gypsy into the narrow mouth of a tributary stream which was not navigable. The Gypsy ran hard aground upon a rock, damaging its rudder and making it necessary to lay to until the high tide so that she might again float free.

The inexperienced pilot is like unto a misguided or vicious leader of men who, loud in self-sufficiency, offers to pilot his followers through treacherous waters. Actually, when the test comes, he directs them toward dangerous shoals upon which they may wreck their lives unless they learn before it is too late that the navigable channel of success lies another way.

The Parable of

THE BROKEN RUDDER

SINCE navigation began, every true sailor has assured himself before setting sail that the rudder of his ship was sound in all its parts. For a ship may be held upon her true course only when the rudder is in proper working order.

Now it so happened that as the false guide was attempting to negotiate a sharp turn in an effort to sail into a narrow tributary of the Shark River, he ran the Gypsy aground, whereupon, reversing the motor, he did back the Gypsy hard upon a rocky ledge.

As it was the time of the outgoing tide, it was apparent that the Gypsy was hard fast until such time as the tides flowed inward again to lift the ship free.

As the tides run, this came to pass, at which time it was discovered that the rudder post and supporting braces were bent in such a way as to render the rudder utterly useless. It was necessary that the rudder be unshipped and repaired before it was possible for the Gypsy to proceed and hold to a true course.

The damaged Gypsy was like unto the person who has no true rudder wherewith to keep his course through the storms of life. Such a one, attempting to steer his frail ship without a belief in the supreme God who causes the sun to shine, the moon to give forth her light, and vessels to be brought safe to port, is truly manning a rudderless ship, whose aimless course must lead him to destruction.

The Parable of

THE
PHOSPHORESCENT WATER

WHILE the Gypsy lay at anchor near the head waters of the Shark River and many leagues from the habitation of the white man, the evening sun sank out of sight behind a cloud of burnished gold.

Soon thereafter twilight descended, and in the twilight, stillness reigned. Later, shadows lengthened in the half-light, and darkness closed about.

Then it was that strange, uncanny night noises began— a splash in the water here, a breaking twig on the bank over there; and a fluttering yonder. The hoot of the owl rent silence and the eyes of the bobcat glowed in unearthly brilliance from the branches of the trees upon the nearby bank.

In the eerie darkness, the surface of the water stirred with a streak of fire, then another and another. Soon the very waters themselves appeared as liquid fire, becoming alternately light, then dark.

This light appeared upon the surface of the water whenever it was disturbed by fishes darting hither and yon. And it was found that the waters could be made to glow with this strange light by agitating them with a rod or with the hand. This curious and beautiful phenomenon is produced by the phosphorescence of the water. Those still waters, running through swamp-land, are highly impregnated with the phosphorus which arises from decomposed subtropical vegetation with which the region abounds.

The unearthly beauty produced from such earthy sources is like unto the accomplishment of many a common-seeming man, a scientist whose gifts do not appear exceptional, a laborer undistinguished from his fellows. Yet out of the ordinary stuff of living, some of these do kindle fires to serve as inspiration to all mankind.

The Parable of

THE SHELL BOX

OW as the Gypsy returned from her journey to the head waters of the Shark River, her course lay almost due south directly to the city of Key West. However, because the barometer was falling rapidly and as the direct course lay through the open waters of the Gulf of Mexico, it was thought best to proceed eastward to the Florida Keys. Thus the Gypsy would be favored by their protection if a storm arose.

In the early afternoon, the Gypsy put in at the small harbor of Matecumbe Key. This Key is but a narrow strip of sand, at no point wider than one hundred feet. From the upper deck of the Gypsy one could watch the giant waves break on the Atlantic side of the Key almost under the forefeet of the ship, and on the opposite side of the Key, though the Gulf of Mexico was calm, yet did the spindrift drive before the wind far into the Gulf, appearing as a mist obscuring the horizon.

31

Through the mist in dim outline, there appeared a tiny island entirely devoid of vegetation. On this island appeared the bulk of a small building or shack. Through powerful binoculars, it was discovered that two human beings moved about on the island. Upon inquiry, it was found that this was their home, that they were husband and wife who sought no companionship with their fellows and were thought to possess some treasure which they guarded carefully at all times.

Inasmuch as this situation appeared to present an interesting problem in human conduct, these island-dwellers were sought out, and after a brief conversation, it was agreed that the treasure which they prized so highly should be brought aboard the Gypsy, and the history thereof related. So it was done, and when the treasure was placed on a table in the Gypsy's cabin, and its wrapping of patchwork quilt removed, it was revealed as an object of wondrous beauty.

The husband was an artisan who wrought in stone, and in earlier years he had traveled far throughout the land, where buildings of unusual beauty were being erected, upon or within which delicate figurines or traceries in stone were to be carved. With the artisan on all of his travels had gone his wife who shared his unusual sense of the beautiful.

In their journeys they had observed upon the shores of the seven seas beautiful shells of every color and in combinations of color. These multi-colored shells so fastened on their imagination that they decided to gather together the most beautiful of them and fashion a treasure chest. By their own words, and who shall doubt it, they searched and labored for seven years.

First they made a box of fine mahogany, selected from among the many beautiful woods of Mexico. It was fashioned thirty-five inches long, twelve inches wide, and ten inches deep. Then they wrought intricate designs upon the wood like unto those which the artisan had traced upon stone. Finally, as they discovered perfect shells to suit their plans, each shell was attached with invisible cement to its proper place within the pattern of the box. When it was finished, it was undoubtedly the most beautiful shell box in all the world.

And they kept it wrapped in a patchwork quilt in a shack upon a desert island.

The keeping of the shell box is like unto the parable recorded in the nineteenth chapter of Luke where it is said that a certain king, upon going to a far country, called his servants unto him, and, delivering to them ten talents of silver, said unto them after this fashion, Go to, now. While I am absent each of you endeavor to produce an increase from the talents which I have placed in your hands, and when I return I will demand an accounting of you.

When the king returned he called his servants unto him. The first servant said, Behold, thy talent hath earned ten. And the king said, Well done, thou good and faithful servant. Thou art rewarded accordingly.

The second servant made answer, Behold, O King, thy talent hath earned five. And the king answered, Well done, thou good and faithful servant. Thou too art rewarded accordingly.

Then the third servant appeared and said, O King, here is thy talent which I have kept hidden in a napkin lest it be stolen or lost, in which case I would have no talent to return to thee.

Then the king condemned the unprofitable servant because he had failed to use that which might have given both pleasure and profit to society.

"The name of this ship was the Gyp

fitting name for a vessel vagabond.''

The Parable of

THE FLOWING SPRING

HE WHO looks upon the map of Florida cannot fail to be impressed with the unusual formation of small islands which extend from the northern limits of Biscayne Bay southward past the city of Key West, a distance in excess of two hundred leagues from one extremity to the other, dividing in their course the Atlantic Ocean from the Gulf of Mexico.

From the days of the Spanish buccaneers, these islands have been known as the Florida Keys. Extending the length of the Keys, within the Gulf of Mexico, is that strip of the Gulf which navigators of sailing ships in olden days called the Spanish Channel. The Spanish Channel acted as a safe passageway for sailing ships by virtue of the breakwater formed by the Keys and also because the prevailing winds were fair abeam north and south for ships sailing through this passage.

Now when the Gypsy was lying at anchor at Matecumbe Key, midway of the north and south extremities of the Keys, a problem arose as to where fresh water might be secured, so that the ship could proceed on her way. It was found that aside from such fresh water as might be caught in receptacles on the roofs of buildings during a rain, the only water available in that vicinity was to be found flowing from a spring on Englishman Island nearby.

This tiny island is only a few acres in extent, located to the Atlantic side of the Keys. At its very heart flows a spring of clear, cold water of sufficient volume to furnish, if need be, all ships sailing that way.

Native tradition has it that this island is the property of an Englishman, a native of the city of London, who retains ownership that this life-saving water may be free to all who come and avail themselves of it. Tradition further states that this lone spring of fresh water in times past saved the lives of many a sailing expedition of bygone days. Now among all the beautiful tropical islands which dot this channel, truly is Englishman Island set apart.

It is like unto the story of the Apostle Paul who, when he journeyed to the city of Athens, found the Athenians worshipping many gods. Whereupon he stood on the top of Mars Hill and declared to the great concourse of people in substance as follows: I perceive you are very religious and worship many gods, yea, even an unknown god, but I am come to declare unto you the only true God in all the universe who is able to give unto you the sustaining water of life which is free for the taking.

The Parable of

THE GREAT STORM

T IS said that only one individual in a million possesses vision and ability above that of the average. Such a one among the million was a man by the name of Flagler.

It was he who conceived the plan for cities on the Florida Keys, and who, by the diligence of his labors, made possible the completion of a railway more than two hundred miles in length, extending from the city of Miami on the north to Key West on the south, interconnecting by causeway and bridge the Keys which lie along the route.

Upon the completion of the railway, certain men, together with their families and friends, established homes upon the previously uninhabited Keys. As the population increased, a highway to bear the vehicle traffic became a necessity. So, over a period of years, bridges were built from Key to Key, and where bridges were

37

impracticable, ferry boats plied their way. Eventually the Florida Keys became a highway for traffic of all sorts, both by railway and by road.

Now it is worthy of note that all the causeways had been built from sand and other materials taken from the bottom of the sea. All bridges were constructed by driving wooden posts into the bottom of the sea and attaching a wooden roadway to the levelled top thereof. For many years, the causeways and bridges rendered valuable service to those who live or traveled upon the Keys.

But there came a time when a great storm arose and grew in violence until one wooden bridge after another was swept away, one causeway after another was spread once more upon the bottom of the sea. Not only were all the works of man destroyed, but man himself, who dwelt within the area, perished in the storm.

Into this desolation came others, men of science and great ability in the planning of permanent things. In due season, they erected, not of sand and wood, but of steel and concrete, a highway extending the entire distance of the Florida Keys. This highway was so constructed that the elements cannot destroy it; neither will time nor tide affect it for many generations.

It is like unto the parable recorded in Holy Writ, of the man who built his house upon the sand which, when the winds descended and the waves beat upon it, was destroyed. But the house which was builded upon a rock withstood the wind and waves, and did not fail.

In turn this parable is like unto the man who builds a character. For is it not true that only character built on the solid rock of a firm belief in an eternal God will withstand the storms of life?

The Parable of

THE BLOW-OUT

WHILE the Gypsy lay at anchor at Matecumbe Key, awaiting an opportune time and tide for proceeding on her course, a desire arose in her passengers to travel by the great new highway to its southern extremity, the city of Key West.

Accordingly the services of a car and driver were secured for the journey. Proceeding southward toward the rising sun of early morning, one beholds many wondrous sights. Not the least of these is the evidence of man's ability to overcome the almost insurmountable obstacles attendant on the construction of such a time-defying highway.

Arriving safely at Key West, it was found that the automobile, having proceeded thus far on a straight course, could be turned only in one direction. Thus if the objective happened to be on the left-hand instead of the right-hand of the road, it was necessary to go completely around a block and approach from the opposite side. This curious state of affairs convinced the driver of the automobile that he must have repairs made enabling the machine to turn both right and left in the approved manner before the return trip. While this operation was in progress, the mechanic informed the driver that the rear tires of his machine were worn so thin that it was dangerous to drive them further. Accordingly the driver stated that he would change them before departing again on the highway.

The return journey was begun, in full confidence that the car's operator had changed the tires according to his word. As the car gained speed crossing Horse Neck Key one of the tires which should have been changed, but was not, suddenly gave way with a loud explosion. The force of the explosion was so great that the machine and all its occupants narrowly escaped being precipitated into the deep waters of the Bay.

Events of this journey are like unto several things. Is not the machine which would turn in only one direction like the stubborn or unreasonable man who, by looking and turning only one direction, stands in the way of his own progress?

Then is not the tire like the person of a violent temper, which manifests itself always at a critical or dangerous period?

And again is not the driver like the slothful and untruthful man who because of these characteristics is willing to endanger even the lives of his fellow-citizens? Yea, verily, a lazy man and a liar are an abomination.

The Parable of

THE PELICAN
WITH ONE WING

WHILE the Gypsy was anchored at Matecumbe Key, awaiting the auspicious hour for sailing, some time was spent angling for the smaller species of fishes. During the period of this so-called "still fishing," many pelicans gathered about, and so fearless were they that they frequently claimed a fish even before it could be landed on deck.

Among these pelicans was one tamer than the others, a pelican possessed of only one wing and therefore unable to fly or dive for its food in the accustomed manner. Because of his handicap, this bird had developed great skill, a quickness and alertness lacking among the other pelicans. Furthermore, the handicapped one had cultivated the friendship of human beings. He was known far and wide by the name of Peter, and there were those who came daily to supply Peter with abundance of food because of his infirmity. Indeed it appeared that Peter, as a member of the pelican family, was happier, better fed, and more prosperous than any of his fellows.

He was like unto the handicapped person who being afflicted by the loss of important faculties uses to the uttermost those faculties remaining to him. Instead of becoming morose or discouraged, he develops himself to a state of usefulness and happiness even beyond that of his fellow associates.

The Parable of

THE ENGINE
WITH A BROKEN CYLINDER

THE Gypsy, not being a sailing ship, is propelled by means of an engine having eight cylinders, and it is through these cylinders that motive power is derived. When all the cylinders function perfectly, working in harmony, the power derived therefrom propels the Gypsy through the water at what is referred to as a maximum cruising speed of twelve miles per hour.

Now as the Gypsy proceeded northward toward Miami, having arrived at the lower reaches of Biscayne Bay, a great noise arose from within the engine indicating that beyond a doubt some essential part had given way. The Gypsy dropped anchor, so that an investigation might be made; whereupon it was discovered that a rocker arm, one of which is attached to the head of each cylinder, had broken. The result was that, whereas the rocker arm clattered with a great noise, the piston within the cylinder did not move. Thus there was no explosion of motor fuel within the cylinder, and thus no power was generated in it. As it was impossible to repair the broken rocker arm upon the high seas, it was decided to disconnect it, for it was only a hindrance and of no value. With one cylinder inactive, the Gypsy proceeded on her way at a speed greatly retarded because the full power of the engine was no longer available.

The Gypsy's engine is like unto a business organization or a church, fraternal, or indeed any organization in which a number of persons function together for the common good of all. When all work together in peace and harmony, and their efforts are properly coordinated, the organization moves forward at the maximum cruising speed. But should there be one among the group who becomes sulky or selfish, or who, for any reason, fails to work harmoniously with his fellows, he retards the progress of the whole group. Like the broken cylinder, he must be either eliminated or brought back into working operation with the rest of the mechanism, lest the whole structure become ineffectual.

The Parable of

THE PUMP

NOW one of the prime necessities of any ship which sails the seas is a goodly supply of fresh water. The Gypsy's water supply was contained within a huge copper tank located within the bow of the ship. The tank was sturdy, strong, built of heavy sheets, with ribs of iron to withstand a heavy pressure of air which, when forced into the tank by means of a pump, caused the water to flow to all parts of the ship through pipes, and from thence to flow as the faucets were opened.

As the Gypsy sailed northward on Biscayne Bay, it was suddenly discovered that when the faucets were opened, no water came forth. Upon investigation it was found that the pump whose function was to maintain a certain pressure of air within the tank had a broken valve. Not only could it supply no air pressure to make the tank function properly, but it could not restrain the air already in the tank from escaping. Thus the tank, filled with an abundance of fresh water, was rendered altogether useless.

The tank is like unto a person of infinite capabilities. He is ready and willing to give all that he has, yet the fulfillment of his function in life depends upon circumstances beyond his control. The valve is like unto the administrator or director of large affairs. If in the crucial hour, he fails, he is responsible not only for rendering his own life useless, but for destroying the effectiveness of the work of others as well.

The Parable of

THE PORTUGUESE
MAN-O'-WAR

THERE is a very peculiar fish which inhabits southern seas, and it is called the Portuguese Man-O'-War.

This fish, which is unlike any other, probably belongs to the jellyfish family, although its characteristics differ greatly even from the jellyfish. Its body is a nebulous mass, six to ten inches long, to which are attached many tentacles varying in length from three to twelve inches. These appear like a series of small serpents as they move through the water.

To the body of the fish, extending upward out of the water, is attached a thin film of tissue which can be inflated or deflated at will. When the film is inflated it becomes a tiny zeppelin, beautifully multi-colored, visible on the surface of the water for a considerable distance.

Now this film serves the purpose of a sail which, by

some miraculous method of construction, assumes a position always broadside to the wind. This film is propelled through the water at a rate of speed sufficient to cause all the tentacles to be extended from the rear as the fish moves forward. Thus do the tentacles come into contact with and capture the small fish which are the food of the Portuguese Man-O'-War. The beauty of the surface portion of this fish contrasts strangely with the almost grotesque ugliness of the remainder of his oddly constructed body. Without his rainbow-colored sail, the Man-O'-War could not navigate. Without his ugly tentacles, he could not gather food to sustain life. Both have their functions necessary to his very existence. One must look, not only to the Man-O'-War's beautiful sails, but to his utilitarian tentacles as well, to discover the meaning of his existence.

Even so, of people and things, one must study the surface, for it has its purpose; then, too, one must look far beneath to discover the whole truth so that right judgment and correct appraisal may be formed.

The Parable of

THE HERMIT CRAB

OW it is a well-known fact that the most curious and amazing things of the world are the creatures of nature which live upon the surface of the earth and within the waters thereof.

Among the most strange is the hermit crab. This creature toils not, neither does he spin. It builds nothing, nor does it leave a monument. It is probably a member of the crayfish family. When it is born, it is deposited in a tiny shell left vacant by another sea animal. As it grows, it seeks larger shells so that by the time it has grown sufficiently to be self-supporting it has discovered and is occupying, perhaps, the shell of the fighting conch. In this home the hermit crab has ensconced himself, but he allows his claws to protrude from the opening in such manner that he can propel himself rapidly over the sand, and thus catch food. Disguised by what appears to be an empty shell, he catches the unwary. Living a life completely devoted to destructive enterprise, having accomplished nothing constructive, the hermit crab constantly preys upon the marine society of which he is a part.

The parasitic hermit crab is like unto the person who goes through life loudly proclaiming that the world owes him a living. He does nothing throughout his lifetime which is worthy of note, or which would entitle him even to live among his fellows. Like the hermit crab, he too will soon pass away, mourned by none; neither will he leave a monument.

The Parable of

THE CAPTAIN WHO
SAILED IN A FOG

UPON the evening of a golden sunset, the Gypsy sailed into the tight little harbor of Eau Gallie, homeward bound. To reach its appointed destination on the evening of the next day, it was determined to take off again at dawn.

So on the following morning, as the rays of the rising sun slanted upward from below the horizon into the fleecy clouds of high heaven, the Gypsy slipped her moorings and sailed away northward.

The barometer was steady and all indications favored a perfect day. However, after the Gypsy had proceeded a short way upon the Indian River, the wind shifted landward off the Atlantic Ocean which at that point lies only a few knots to the starboard as a ship sails northward. The wind, which was not violent, carried with it a dense fog which, in a moment of time, enveloped the

Gypsy, limiting visibility to a distance not exceeding fifty feet.

As the Captain continued to sail, apprehension came upon his passengers lest, in the midst of the fog, they meet disaster by running upon a rock, sand-bar, or other obstruction. Whereupon the Captain was approached and spoken to in this wise, "Why do we proceed under the circumstances, when the fog is upon us and we cannot observe the channel, neither can we see any great distance?"

To this the Captain replied, "Look here upon the chart, and observe the compass. The chart states the depth of water at all times and in all places. Providing I continue to follow the directions indicated, I shall not come in contact with shoals or shallows, but will sail safely as long as I have sufficient visibility to observe ships approaching from the opposite direction."

The Captain is like unto the man who, having established his goal, taking into consideration all contingencies and preparing himself for the journey by much learning, proceeds along the course which he has laid out. He fears not, neither does he waver, nor permit himself to be dissuaded from his course, but in confidence proceeds to his objective.

The Parable of

THE SUNSET
THAT WAS LOST

NOW as the Gypsy was sailing north on the Halifax River, a narrow stream wooded on either bank with royal palms, palmettos and cyprus assembled by nature in such manner as to present a picture of beauty beyond description, the afternoon faded away and the evening sunset approached. The sun nearing the horizon became large and luminous, but ceased to be dazzling to the eyes.

Over the landscape to the west, toward the setting sun, there arose a mist from the lowlands which, meeting the sun's rays, appeared to break into a fan-like perfect half-circle, extending from horizon to horizon on either side of the sun. The circle was broken into five triangular sections on either side, and in each section appeared all the colors of the spectrum — an effect which man attempted to reproduce in the beautiful colored lighting of Chicago's Century of Progress Exposition.

Truly the most glorious sunset they had ever beheld, the Gypsy's passengers stood spellbound. One held a camera awaiting the moment of greatest beauty to secure a lasting record of this magnificent phenomenon. But before a picture record was made, the Gypsy sailed behind a grove of royal palms, which, interposed between the sunset and the Gypsy, made it impossible to secure a picture. When the grove of palms was passed, the picture had vanished, the sunset faded into twilight.

The lost sunset is like unto the young person of unusual promise, and great ability, possessing the physical and mental training to set an important mark in the world, and yet who allows his golden moments of opportunity to slip by one by one. His talent and his promise, all unused, at last fade from him into the gray twilight of the years.

The Epilogue of

A DREAM COME TRUE

NOW the Gypsy at the end of the appointed time for the vagabond voyage, put into her home port, having brought her passengers safely back to the world of reality out of the world of dreams.

Refreshed and happy, having filled their minds and hearts with memories to be treasured for a lifetime, the family thus privileged to realize their dream came back to take up familiar duties, and to walk within the accustomed pattern of their ways.

With no regret that the journey was past, but with full contentment in the joys which they shared, the family set out to do gladly those tasks which lay next to hand. They remembered and rejoiced in the words spoken in Ecclesiastes, whereby we are told in part, "For everything there is a season, and a time for every purpose under heaven: a time to plant and a time to pluck up that which is planted; a time to weep and a time to laugh; a time to cast away stones and a time to gather stones together; a time to seek and a time to lose; a time to keep and a time to cast away; a time to keep silence and a time to speak."

So be it.